The Absence of Fatherhood is No Joke

By

Dennis L. Aikens

1stBooks – rev. 10/17/01

In Memory of:

Grandma Hattie, Aunt Betty,
Aunt Iola, and Isaiah

This book is dedicated to my
wife and four sons:
Beverly, Delandrian, Dennis Jr., Derrin, and
Derrick
And to my mother, Barbara

To the person who never stopped
believing in me

In the name of my Lord and Savior Jesus Christ
To Whom Much Is Given Much is Required.

"Gotta Give It Up"

Table of Contents

Introduction

Though my father and mother forsake me, the Lord will receive me. Psalm 27:10

I remember growing up when children with fathers would tease other children about the fact that they had no father in their home. I often remember being asked where my Daddy was, followed by taunting statements such as, "Oh, he ran off with another woman" or "Your mama kicked him out because he can't keep a job." Well, to many children that was just not funny, and it was especially not funny to me.

I was born to a single mother in the mid 1950's, in the city housing project of Yamacraw Village, located on the west side of the coastal city of Savannah, Georgia. The first six years of my life were spent here, where my mother and I shared a three-bedroom apartment with my grandfather, grandmother, two aunts, one uncle, and four cousins. I remember very little from that season, but I was told my mother was often away being treated for a physical ailment.

My grandmother, whom we called "Momma," was very visible in the first years of my life and she instilled in me many of the positive principles and qualities that any child needs to start his race in life. She was truly a God-fearing person. Then, at the age of seven, I was reunited with my mother, and we moved into our first apartment together. My mother was a beautiful woman who had a gift from God to love people. She would always try to help anyone in need. Women played a great role in my development because, there were few men around in my family. Later in life my aunt would teach me my love for business.

After several months in that first apartment we moved to Hitch Village, another city housing project located on the east side of Savannah. Hitch Village would be the place that would define my life for many years to come.

This would also be the place, though I did not realize it until years later, where God would begin to mold me for the type of leadership in the church that awaits me as you read this book.

Chapter One

It Is Just Not Funny

He will turn the hearts of the fathers to their
children, and the hearts of the children to their
fathers; or else I will come and strike the land
with a curse. (Malachi 4:6)

Immediately after my mom and I moved
into Hitch Village, I was greeted by the
"welcoming committee" who came to check
out the new kid on the block. This is what they
must have seen: a slender, seven-year-old
African-American kid who dressed "nerdy,"
with "high water" pants and skunk shoes. I was
a kid who looked and dressed like a "Mama's
Boy." I was a kid with no father and no
brothers and sisters. To the welcoming
committee, I was considered easy prey.

For the next several months that small group
prepared me for years of being bullied, picked
on and ridiculed. To the average kid growing
up in Hitch Village in the 1960's and early

1

Dennis L. Aikens

1970's, I was considered to be weak and an easy target because I didn't have the support system that many of them had. But in my weakness, I did not realize that God was making me strong. I did not realize there were people in my family who knew God and were praying for me. I was skating on the prayers of some of my ancestors. For the Bible says in Proverbs 15:8, *"But the prayer of the upright, pleases him."* For years I dealt with being intimidated, threatened, and bullied because I had no father, sisters, or brothers to give me strength. Psalms 68:5a says, *"God will be a father to the fatherless,"* and God was my strength and guided me towards my destiny. God led me through obstacles, attacks, and confrontations. I was fatherless and a prey to many. But though I lacked physical strength and was labeled weak in the ghetto, I was exactly what God wanted.

The Bible speaks about how God glories in situations like these. Gideon, in the Book of Judges, and David, in the Book of I Samuel and I Kings, knew the very stuff that leaders are made from. For the Apostle Paul says in I

2

Corinthians 1:27-28, "*but God chose the foolish things of the world to shame the wise; God chose the weak things of the world to shame the strong. He chose the lowly things of this world and the despised things and the things that are not to nullify the things that are so that no one may boast before him.*" God wants the glory and He can't get it until we are empty before Him.

Paul speaks about a weakness he had and how God wanted it that way in order for the world to see the power of God working in the midst of and in spite of all our weaknesses. Paul states in 2 Corinthians 12:7-10 that *God, to keep me from becoming conceited because of these surpassingly great revelations, there was given me a thorn in my flesh, a messenger of Satan, to torment me. Three times I pleaded with the Lord to take it away from me. But he said to me, My grace is sufficient for you, for my power is made perfect in weakness. Therefore, I will boast all the more gladly about my weaknesses so that Christ's power may rest on me. That is why, for Christ's sake, I delight in weaknesses, in insults, in hardships,*

3

in persecutions, in difficulties, 'for when I am weak, then I am strong'."

All of this is great and encouraging when you come into the knowledge of the word of God. But, as a little boy in Hitch village without a father for strength, security and guidance, it was hard to feel encouraged. I did not know the word of God. I did not know God was molding me. For those of us without a father, life could be brutal and very painful.

Few Fathers in the Village

Hitch Village was a great place to grow up in spite of some of the bad experiences I endured. Once the kids on my block got to know me, we all became friends and family. There was one thing most of us had in common: we did not have a father in the home. Some fathers lived across town, some fathers lived out of town—and then there were those of us who did not even know our father's names, who never saw our fathers once while growing up.

Early on, I did not understand that a part of me was missing. But as I approached age ten and beyond, I began to realize that lacking a father was not normal. I would occasionally ask my mother who my father was, and it would cause her so much pain that she would react in anger. I always felt that my mother thought that I was slighting her and that I was unappreciative. After all, she was there. She was the one raising me and no one was forcing him, my father, to stay away from his son. But my mother never could understand that it was

5

something deep in my soul driving me to understand who I was and where I came from. It was bigger than knowing whom my father was. It was about knowing where I came from so that I could find out where I was going and who I could become. And the key to that is knowledge.

According to the Bible, we can know ourselves through our generations of fathers. Your own father may be a poor excuse for a father, but his father might have been saintly: a lover of God, and all that is right. Information about a child's father or mother should never be withheld from them by the other parent or any other family member, regardless of its nature. That is a promise that should not be broken to any child.

There were some kids around my way that had fathers, and some of them became neighborhood fathers. They interacted with most of the kids and made us all feel good. But the interaction was limited because those few fathers had to work to take care of their families. As I look back on that time, I thank God for those precious moments that I had with those two or three neighborhood fathers. There was one father who played basketball in the park with many of the kids in the village in his spare time, another who enjoyed dropping us off at Boy Scout camp sites in his pick-up, and yet another who played cards with the kids. That was pretty much it, other than the boyfriends of the mothers in the neighborhood. It wasn't pretty, but we all survived.

Too Many Crippled Children

The absence of fathers is crippling our homes and our society. There are too many crippled children walking around, and it's just not funny anymore. In truth, it was never funny.

These are children crippled in their minds, in their spirits, and in their souls. They are also crippled in their self-esteem, their morals, their hopes, their confidence and their lack of knowledge of who they are. Too many of our children are hurting on the inside because their fathers chose to cripple them instead of empowering, girding, and loving them. Their fathers chose instead to leave them at the mercy of Satan, and we all know Satan has no mercy.

This crippling effect is being passed onto generations as we watch our children beget their own children. Now it's *their* offspring who are made cripple as they watch their fathers disappear. One by one, they fall.

After the father has disappeared, most children are left with a single mother, and some of these parents are too weak to raise a child alone. Many of these mothers are so young, they have not matured themselves. The last thing they need is the responsibility of raising a child. Hence, the child is left dangling between grandmother, mother and other relatives, rarely stable. He or she grows up with a poor self-identity, trusting few people and never feeling secure. Meanwhile, the father that walked away or the father that just couldn't get along with the mother is nowhere to be found. If only he would make a brief appearance, or send some support money to ease the financial burdens of the home, then some comfort could be found and questions answered. But there is never a word.

It's Just Not Normal

In our society the phrase "I raised five children by myself," or "I grew up with seven brothers and sisters without a dad," is considered the norm. No matter how those families turn out, such arrangements cannot be considered normal. It is not biblical. "*God made man in His own image and because God did not want man to be alone and He knew man needed help, He made woman.*" (Genesis 1:27; 2:18-22.)

The Bible says in Genesis 1:27 b&c, "*in the image of God he created Him; male and female he created them.*" Genesis 1:28 says, "*God blessed them and said to them, be fruitful and increase in number; fill the earth and subdue it.*" God continued setting up the family in Genesis 3 after Adam and Eve disobeyed Him. He said to Eve, "*I will greatly increase your pains in childbearing; with pain you will give birth to children. Your desire will be for your husband, and he will rule over you.*" With this proclamation, God bespeaks what is normal. Dad and mom are supposed to be together.

9

The New Testament again emphasizes God's plan in Ephesians 5:22-32, *"Wives, submit to your husbands as to the Lord. For the husband is the head of the wife as Christ is the head of the church, His body, of which he is the Savior. Now as the church submits to Christ, so also wives should submit to their husbands in everything. Husbands, love your wives, just as Christ loved the church and gave himself up for her. To make her holy, cleansing her by the washing with water through the word, and to present her to himself as a radiant church, without stain or wrinkle or any other blemish, but holy and blameless."*

It is thus normal when two Christians of the opposite sex love each other, get married, have children, and raise their children according to the complete counsel of God's word. Normal is when both parents are in the home instructing, directing and caring for their children. No other lifestyle is normal, regardless of what occurs everyday in the real world.

Chapter Two

We Have Not Many Fathers

*I will be a father to you, and you will be my
sons and daughters, says the Lord Almighty.* (II
Corinthians 6:18)

What is a "father?" Why is his absence
causing so much hurt and pain in our society,
especially in the African American community?

The American Heritage Dictionary defines
"father" as "a male parent who functions in a
paternal capacity with regard to another; a man
who creates, founds or originates something,
and also accepts responsibility for that which
he creates." The same dictionary defines
fatherhood as the condition of "being a father."

I conclude that there are many boys and men
who are fathers because they created a baby,
but they are not living up to the condition of
being a father as in *fatherhood* because they are
not accepting responsibility for what they have
created. Children are being birthed in homes

11

where the father is absent literally and/or spiritually. Immediately the house is wounded because a major part of it is missing, the mother is hurting, and the devil sees all.

The father, because he was created in the image of God (Genesis 1:26), is supposed to be the covering for his children from the evils of the world. Instead, he has left his children to be open targets. Then God said, *"Let us make man in our image, in our likeness, and let them rule over the fish of the sea and the birds of the air, over the livestock, over all the earth, and over all the creatures that move along the ground."*

Many mothers have done a remarkable job of raising children all by themselves. Some have not done so well, but even less successful mothers have done better than the absent fathers. They *tried*. They tried to make a difference, even though there is no substitute for an absent father. There is only so much a single mother can do for a child, alone. Absent fathers have left too many mothers out of the order with God's program.

Fathers were created to be the head of the household—to be the guide, the provider, the protector and the teacher. The mother's role is just as important, but one without the other leaves an unfulfilled, sometimes angry child to roam the streets. Society—*we*—ultimately pay the price, as fatherless children often release their frustrations upon us. Because of the great challenges single parenthood creates, it is crucial that these mothers find God early in their children's life so that they can get the spiritual help they need from Jesus.

Jesus said in Mark 10:14b-15, "*Let the little children come to me, and do not hinder them, for the kingdom of God belongs to such as these. I tell you the truth, anyone who will not receive the kingdom of God like a little child will never enter in.*" At the brink of this new millennium, men across America are being challenged to get their house in order. God is calling on fathers everywhere to receive the blessing that has always been theirs, and to strike down every generational curse hindering their daily walk with God.

When God called out Abraham in Genesis, 12th chapter, He was seeking demonstrations of obedience and faith. Thousands of years later, God still calls on these two qualities from men.

"The Lord had said to Abraham, leave your country, your people and your father's household and go to the land I will show you. I will make you into a great nation and I will bless you; I will make your name great and you will be a blessing. I will bless those who bless you and whoever curses you I will curse and all peoples on earth will be blessed through you." (Genesis 12:1-3)

Abraham's obedience and faith established a standard for fathers for generations to come, but many descendants from him broke the pattern, resulting in weakness and dysfunction. Sin reestablished its grip in the homes where the father was not there, or he was not operating as the priest of his home. So, for generations after God established his covenant with Abraham, God has had to watch man after man fail to be the father God has ordained him to be.

I know, of course, that there were good God-fearing fathers then and good God-fearing fathers now, but the numbers are not enough.

God has to be a little disappointed in those who have fathered children and left them to be raised only by a mother who lacks the paternal skills necessary to train a boy how to become a man. A mother can teach a boy how to respect womanhood, but she can never truly teach a boy how to *be a man*. That is a father's job.

Someone To Look Up To

A good, God-fearing father who is resourceful, reliable, and a Promise Keeper will send a positive message to his children. In deed, not word, he will say to his children: "I am here for you and you can look up to me, always. When you are in trouble, I will be by your side. When you are sick, I will be by your side. When you need a push or your confidence stirred up, just look for me and I will give you strength."

This unwavering commitment parallels with what Jesus said in Matthew 28:20 after He had given the charge to the disciples to take the gospel to all nations leading them to God's saving grace and baptizing them in the name of the Father and the Son and Holy Spirit. Jesus said: *"Surely I am with you always, to the very end of the age."* Too many children today, regardless of race, do not know who is with them. They have no role models, no strong leader, no one to answer their many questions. Fathers are absent. Mothers are too busy trying to make ends meet. Thus, too many of our children desperately seek a hero. But they are finding the wrong heroes. A father should be a child's greatest hero because he is made in God's image, and he should possess many of the divine qualities of God.

Who becomes your male mentor if there are no father or brothers around? In my case, there were a couple of young men that saw my need and potential to be anything that I wanted to be, despite the overwhelming odds. One of these good men adopted me as a little brother. He took me everywhere—on dates with his girlfriend, to basketball and football games, and even to the movies. He took my friends and me fishing and crabbing. He let me drive his station wagon when I was twelve or thirteen years old. And, importantly, he engaged me in deep talks about life, school and girls. He was a breath of fresh air to me at times when I really needed the oxygen.

The other mentor was my basketball and baseball coach. Here was a man who believed in me when I began playing recreational sports. He saw something in my nine-year-old self that I didn't even know I had: competitiveness. I could hardly dribble a basketball, and was scared when the coach started coming to my house begging my mother to let me play on his teams every year. I became his project. He was determined to make me a good ball player. I always thank God for him. He taught me toughness, to fear no one or nothing.

The heroes that too many of our children are finding are drug pushers, pimps, prostitutes, convicts and other folk who don't know God, or don't want to know him "yet." They give our children false love, false hope, and a listening ear—the very same things that Satan offers us.

The time has come when we as fathers must get to a mirror and evaluate thoroughly what we see in its reflection. Do we see what God made us to be? If not, then we must go and correct ourselves by allowing the Holy Spirit to come in and clean up the mess we have made. Then we need to go back and look in that mirror again. It is not enough to see someone "as good as the guy next door." No, we must put pressure on ourselves to raise the standard of manhood and fatherhood in our society. We must keep looking and looking until we like what we see in the name of Jesus.

When We Begin To Like What We See

We cannot like seeing ourselves as neglecting our children. We cannot be happy about running the streets on our wife, or spending money in the street when there are bills to be paid. How can we like seeing someone who does not acknowledge God as the head of his life? But once we, as fathers, confront and rebuke our sins and recognize that we need to know God and his plan for our life, then the healing can begin.

Some fathers must be told repeatedly who they are and what authority they possess. There are qualities that are hidden, and God will not allow them to come forth until the men have gotten right with God. God wants fathers to get in order, to shed some things that are keeping them from unrevealed mysteries, promises and blessings. Time is running out, and God is getting impatient with selfish fathers who are blind. Only when fathers open their eyes and ears will God commit to them and trust them. Then fathers will begin to discipline themselves for God's approval. That is when we will begin to like what we see; when we go out of our way to make God smile about us.

In essence we are saying to God, "See Daddy, I am doing what you told me to do and I like it." We should *want* to be good fathers because God is a good father. There should be a sense of pride in our ability to take care of our children, to protect them and mold them into normal and productive adults. There are some animals, elephants and apes for example, that take better care of their young than some human fathers. Yet God gave us the command in Genesis 1:28 to *"fill the earth and subdue it. Rule over the fish of the sea and the birds of the air and over every living creature that moves on the ground.*"

Taking Care of You

Your children are you, made again. If you like yourself, you wash yourself when you are dirty, feed yourself when you are hungry, and clothe yourself when you are naked, then you must like what you have created all over again: your children. They deserve better than what a lot of fathers have given them. It hurts to see a hungry child. It hurts to see a sick child. And it hurts to see a child that does not know who he is. A child with no self-identity inherently lacks self-esteem. This is the child who wears nothing but emptiness on his face—perhaps the saddest spectacle in the world.

It is so important for fathers to know *themselves* before they start creating replicas of themselves. There must be inner peace and a sense of wholeness within a person before he can effectively deal with a new generation (I use the masculine case here because the subject is fathers, although these guiding principles certainly apply to mothers, as well). When a person feels whole, he takes care of his details. He cares about educating himself or learning a trade so that he can secure a job and take care of himself. He cares about how he looks, how he feels, where he goes, and what he does. In essence, when a father cares about all of these things, then and only then will he be able to lovingly care about the next versions of himself: his sons and his daughters.

Caring for this new generation should be more of a joy than a challenge because you are experienced now. You *know* what to do and what not to do. You *know* what roads to travel and what roads to avoid. You are the master of which way to go. So, it should not be hard to guide yourself again, in the form of your children. Taking care of you again is all about love for yourself. If you love yourself, you will love what you have created.

Jesus told husbands to love their wives as they love themselves. Ephesians 5:28-30 says, *"In His same way, husbands ought to love their wives as their own bodies."* He who loves his wife loves himself. After all, no one ever hated his own body, but he feeds and cares for it, just as Christ does the church. For we are members of his body. Similarly, we should love our children as we do our own bodies because our children come from our own bodies. They are us all over again and if we love ourselves, we should love and take care of them.

Do It Because We Love Jesus

Loving our children and being there for them is not only an expression of our love for ourselves, but also of our great love for Jesus. Jesus cared so much for us that he died for us and hence paid an awful penalty for our sins. He did not walk away from his purpose. He did not abandon his responsibility. He paid the price and stayed right where God wanted him to stay in order for us to be delivered and justified. If we would love Jesus the way that Jesus loves us, then we would be able to keep his precepts and examples when it comes to loving others, especially our children.

"Simon, son of John, do you truly love me more than these?" Jesus asked Peter after his

resurrection, in John 21:15-17. *"Yes Lord,"* Peter said. *"You know that I love you ..."* Jesus said, *"take care of my lambs."* The third time He said to him, *"Simon, son of John, do you love me?"* Peter was hurt, because Jesus asked him of his love this third time. Peter said, *"Lord you know all things; you know that I love you."* Jesus then said, *"Feed my sheep."*

Jesus is saying to fathers as well as to pastors: *if you love me then take care of my sheep.* His sheep are not only the members of his church body, but are also the innocent children of our creation who need to be loved and cared for.

The only way that we as fathers can feed the sheep is for us to participate in the lives of our flock. We cannot be absent and feed them at the same time. This is not a joke. This is serious business.

Countless numbers of our children cannot fly into their true destiny because they need a strong, God-fearing father in their lives. There are other children who overcome this dysfunction and go on to become whole and successful in life. But too many, like the loggerhead turtle, never make it into the ocean. They need that fatherly protection, that paternal guidance, and that spiritually wise counsel. The father's absence is critical and paralyzing; it is time that they come back home.

Chapter Three

Fatherless While In the Womb

*The word of the Lord came to me, saying,
before I formed you in the womb, I knew you,
before you were born, I set you apart; I
appointed you as a prophet to the nations.*
(Jeremiah 1:4-5)

It is an awesome thing for a father to be able
to say that he knew his child while he or she
was in the womb. To be able to say, "while
your mother was carrying you during those
nine months, not only did your mother know
you, but I, your father, knew you too," is a
powerful feeling. It is a powerful thing to say,
"I took care of your mother when she was up,
because that affected you. I took care of her
when she was down, because that too affected
you. The happier she was and the more
comfortable she was, the healthier you were."

It is extremely important that fathers touch
their children while they are in the womb by

touching the mother's stomach and body. Holding that mother's hand gives a sense of unity and security to that unborn, but living child. Positive words of life must be spoken to that child in the womb in order to build his character and self-esteem.

Proverbs 25:11 says, "*a word aptly spoken is like apples of gold in settings of silver.*" This scripture is simply saying: words can hurt or heal. They can empower or they can destroy. They can uplift or they can tear down. Wise use of the power of words leads one to know the importance of timing: when to speak, what to say, and how to say it. Providing for his unborn child is also very important for a father to do. The mother must be healthy in order to have a healthy child. A father must ensure that the mother receives nutritious food, proper health care, clothing, shelter and good hygiene during her pregnancy. An unborn child's needs exceed the mere physical attention. It is important that a well-defined spiritual environment be established while that child is in the womb if we want that child to enter into the world with a heart for Christ.

Hannah, in the Book of I Samuel, illustrates a good example of this principle. Hannah was barren, but wanted a male child in the worst way. She loved the Lord mightily and lived everyday for Him. One day she prayed to the Lord in I Samuel 1:10-11 and the Lord answered her prayer.

It is a fact that while she carried her son, Samuel, he had a well-defined spiritual environment because Hannah had no other Gods before her. She made a vow to God that she would present her son to Him to serve God all the days of his life. Before you can present anything or anybody to God you must first ready yourself to meet Him.

Millions Didn't Make It

There have been literally millions of fathers who did not make it or were absent while that child was in the womb. It is unfortunate to say millions didn't make it, but I'm glad I was one of the fathers who did. I will never leave a child of mine fatherless while he or she is in the womb because that is the child's foundation and beginning. All children need to know who their father is to them: he is their strength, their provider, their protection and their spiritual guide. They need to feel his presence, the way we, as children of God, feel God's presence. The more a father's presence is felt, the stronger his child will be.

Psalms 31:20 says, "*in the shelter of your presence you hide them from the intrigues of men.*" In other words, God's presence is like shelter from the wickedness of the world.

As a Father, your presence is very important regardless if the child is in the womb or not, but when you are not there you cannot make a difference, while your child develops in the womb. Your child cannot feel you. Your child cannot hear you, or sense you in any way. Your child starts out in life with a void, being fatherless in the womb. He has been crippled by your absence, in the water. By the time your child is born, his chances of social and spiritual survival have been diminished greatly. His chances of being successful in life have been dampened by the fact that the person who is supposed to be his mentor and his strength is not there. Why are they not there? Why didn't they make it?

Why does being responsible for your children make some men do not want anything to do with their child? Relationship problems, breakup or divorce should have nothing to do with the father being there for their child. What happens between the father and the mother is no excuse for the father's abandonment of his child.

Some Will Survive No Matter What

Some children, because of various factors, will survive being fatherless in the womb no matter what. Many will survive because of their genes, some because of their social environment, and some because God predestined it to be so. Romans 8:29-30 says, *"for those God foreknew he also predestined to be conformed to the likeness of his Son, that he might be the first born among many brothers and those he predestined, he also called; those he called, he also justified; those he justified, he also glorified."*

29

God can take somebody that the world says is no good or doesn't have a chance, and He will bless them and care for them until that perfect moment. Then God will magnify them for His own glory and honor.

This Is Just How God Works

God wants to be the focus of the world's attention; that is why he uses people who will make Him look good. God wants the world to look at us, but then see God. The world looks at our shortcomings and our weaknesses and then watches how God puts His anointing on us, nullifying our defects. Then the world must recognize that only an awesome God can change and glorify somebody that is defected. God is in the business of using weak people, people who started out in a lowly estate. He will make great things come from them. God has a harder time using people who are too self-confident because sometimes they forget the source of their help. IT COMES FROM THE LORD!

Thus, many of you who were fatherless from the womb and survived were predestined by God to do so. Some of you made it because there was somebody who prayed for you or somebody who helped you along the way. Somebody cared enough—a stepfather, an uncle or a family friend—to make sure that you were escorted through those years that would either make you or break you. Far too many children emerge into adulthood with scars and broken places, but they still make it. A real, spirit-filled father would have greatly eased the way for some of these children to make it through. Nothing can take the place of the confidence that a child gets from having a father in his life. A father who cares regardless of whether or not he is still with the child's mother. He wants to be involved in his child's life. He wants to be that positive force that guides his child through everything that the world will place before him.

Dennis L. Aikens

Chapter Four

Fathering After You Leave

Fathers, do not exasperate your children; instead bring them up in the training and instruction of the Lord. (Ephesians 6:4)

The responsibility of nurturing children in the faith is fixed squarely on the shoulders of Christian fathers, whether they are in the home with their children or not. If a father is in order with God, he will have the greatest impact on his children because Christian children are taught to understand the magnitude of the father-child relationship as revealed in God's relationship with those of us who have accepted His son, Jesus Christ, as our personal savior. Those fathers who have not turned their lives over to God must also be very involved in nurturing their children from the inside or the outside.

Obviously, mothers will have much to do with the nurturing and training of their children, but fathers who relinquish this duty entirely to mothers do so in clear violation of New Testament teaching.

Many of our children are hurting because they have no instructions and no guidance. The majority has no father in their home. If fathers outside the home would embrace their responsibilities, many of our children would know what is expected of them. Fathers inside or outside the homes must understand that fathering involves mostly training. "Training" is the Greek work *paideia*, which denotes a combination of instruction, discipline, and personal guidance.

Proverbs 22:6 says, *"Train a child in the way he should go and when he is old he will not turn from it."* Our society cannot afford to lose any more children because of a lack of training. Daddies must attend to their children at all costs and begin to show them the way, teaching them the good from the bad. Fathers can spare their children much grief later in life if they will correct and guide them in their younger years. When fathers do not come back to father their children, they create a "laissez-faire" atmosphere of parenthood: "Let them do as they choose." That type of parenthood can contribute to trouble and unhappiness in the lives of the children, and sometimes lead to their untimely death. Proverbs 19:18 confirms this by telling us to "*discipline your son, for in that there is hope; do not be a willing part to his death.*"

Nobody Can Do It Better

Stepfathers and boyfriends who are biblically grounded are probably the next best thing to a biological father in helping to raise children. Children need that male physical presence, and in many cases these men do a better job than the biological father ever could. This still does not dismiss the fact that the true father can do the best job in raising his children, once he gets his heart right with God.

Nobody can replace what a child feels naturally inside of him knowing that his father is right there by his side. Nobody can stand in that father's place when he is in place doing the right things for his children. Fathers are special to their children because children have an uncanny sense of wanting to know their real fathers—especially when they are absent. Proverbs 17:6b says, *"Parents are the pride of their children."* Nothing less than knowing who produced them will do for most children because they want to know who they are. Many children discover the attributes and characteristics they get from their mother, but when Daddy is not there they never learn answers to the sometimes forbidden questions. Nobody can answer those questions better than you, the father, for it is your qualities that your child inherits. NOBODY CAN BE BETTER THAN YOU.

From The Outside Looking In

Too many fathers who leave their responsibilities behind, in terms of their children, must find a way to look back and touch their lives. Fathers who stay outside their children's lives create offsprings with little self-esteem, children who don't like themselves because they feel rejected by their father. These

35

children ask themselves, "What's wrong with me?" and "What did I do to make him not want to be with me?" and "Why won't he come get me or see about me?"

Over and over these children replay these same questions in their minds as they grow up and their fathers stay on the outside not looking in. Frustrated and full of anger, these children wonder: "What kind of man would walk away forever, never caring enough to stop and see about his child?" Even though you are on the outside, how can you not look in every now and then to give your child financial support, paternal companionship and fatherly and spiritual strength? How can you be so insensitive to the needs of your innocent children? Now, that's just not funny. That's disgraceful.

It's disgraceful because fathers should have enough compassion not to leave their babies out in the open for predators to devour them. When fathers abandon their babies, they leave them for Satan to establish his will in their lives, leading them on to years of misery, despair and certain spiritual or even physical death.

If You Have To Leave

Children have no say so in whether or not their parents stay together. They did not ask to come into this world, but yet in many cases they are abandoned to fend for themselves with one parent. Usually that one parent is the mother. In many cases, children are born out of wedlock to teenage mothers and fathers who are not married. After the first serious argument or financial struggle, the relationship is over and the father is usually the one that steps off the scene.

If the father has to leave, he must swallow his pride, rise above his anger, and focus on the fact that the child he left behind is his. He must act responsibly in caring for and loving that innocent child.

I remember when I began to wonder why my father never came around. What happened between him and my mother? What did she do so wrong? What did he do so wrong? Why did he not want to see me? What did I do wrong? Was he ashamed of me because I was not what he expected? I had so many questions, but I never got any answers—especially from my mother. She was hurt by my father, that was obvious. This was one of the reasons why I always tried to make her happy. I did things to make her proud of me, like making good grades and staying out of trouble. But these accomplishments did little to ease her pain, and her pain affected me tremendously. She would drown herself in alcohol and tears. Sometimes, along with a few friends, she would be up all night long crying in pain. I would lie in my bed trying to shut out the crying, but sometimes I too would cry all night wishing my father would come by to see me. I was mad with him for deserting me, but I still wanted him to come see me.

Then it happened. One day, out of nowhere, came my father. He was a tall, good-looking man with a gold tooth. I was about ten-years-old when he showed up. He asked my mother if he could take me to see his mother. I cautiously went with him. When we finally got to his mother's house off of East Broad Street, and very close to where I lived, someone shouted to my father that his brother was in a fight down the street. I spent the only day I had with my father waiting for him to return from rescuing his brother from that fight. What a bust! He took me back home and I never saw him again for the rest of my life.

Deuteronomy 4:9 says, *"Only be careful, and watch yourselves closely so that you do not forget the things your eyes have seen or let them slip from your heart as long as you live. Teach them to your children and to their children after them."* In other words, if you, as a father, were raised right as a child being taught the righteousness of God, it is your duty to be careful and remember what you were taught, and teach your children. Even if a father was not raised in a home under the influence of God, there should be a natural instinct to protect and care for a child that belongs to him. So if you must leave, if you just got to go, please remember the children.

You can still be a father after you leave. You can still be a positive influence in the life of your children even if you and their mother cannot be a family. Your child deserves you regardless if it's from a distance. And for those fathers who commit themselves to fathering after they leave, our society and our communities benefit from their commitment.

Chapter Five

How It Is Affecting Us

For I, the Lord your God, am a jealous God,
punishing the children for the sin of the fathers
to the third and the fourth generation of those
who hate me, but showing love to a thousand
generations of those who love me and keep my
commandments. (Exodus 20:5b)

When daddy is gone, a whole lot of people are affected.

It all begins with the children. Their lives will never be the same as long as their father remains absent. On the outside it can appear that their situation of being fatherless is okay, but nobody knows the deep things that those children are dealing with in their minds and in their hearts. These deep things can get out of control as they grow up and evolve into sexual immorality, homosexuality, spousal abuse, and child abuse or child molestation. The feelings of being neglected and unwanted can trigger hatred and anger that is taken out on society.

These feelings encourage some children to become bullies in their neighborhoods and in their schools. Some children may eventually become robbers, burglars, murderers or drug dealers. Then there are those that become timid and afraid to interact with others because they did not have that strong male figure showing them the way, giving them a sense of confidence to deal with people who they encounter on a daily basis. Many of these children become introverts. They conceal their thoughts and their feelings inward. This can cause children to become very dangerous when someone gets too close, because they have a problem resolving issues and conflicts, as well as problems with intimacy. These are children who have had few experiences in human relationships and problem solving because they have always been to themselves.

The absence of fathers in many children's lives not only causes many children to become dysfunctional, it can hinder them from becoming what God intended them to be.

Psalm 127:3-5 says, *"Sons are the heritage from the Lord, children a reward from him. Like arrows in the hands of a warrior are sons born in one's youth. Blessed is the man whose quiver is full of them. They will not be put to shame when they contend with their enemies in the gate."*

Too Many Mothers Are Still Suffering

Mothers raising children by themselves are a special breed. Their whole life changes after they have that first child and again after that child's father leaves. It does not matter who was to blame for the separation; the fact still remains that the mother in most cases will raise that child by herself. Unfortunately, most mothers are not equipped, nor prepared to handle raising children alone. This challenge affects them emotionally, psychologically, socially, and financially.

Some mothers let this situation get the best of them. They lose their self-respect and allow themselves to go down. There are cases where mothers just cannot take it anymore, leaving

43

their children to be raised by relatives or foster care. Then there are cases where mothers stay with their children, but let immoral vices such as drugs, alcohol, and too many men lower her standards of living. Her children, who witness this lifestyle, become discouraged, judgmental, and confused. The only role model parent they have is their mother, yet she has disappointed them just like that absent father. There are mothers who abuse their children as a result of the hatred they have for their children's father. The father hurt the mother in their love relationship, leaving her in a scornful way. Tragically, it is sometimes the people closest to her who receive their mother's wrath—her children. She has the mistaken belief that to relieve her own suffering, the children must suffer too. Finally, there are those mothers who do not leave their children or who do not succumb to immoral vices, yet still suffer because it is just not normal to raise children with one parent in the home.

It is unfortunate that some people take advantage of single mothers raising their children. This is true especially in an economically deprived environment such as a housing project. There were times, I know, that if there had been a man or a father around my home, some folks would not have been as brave as they let on. There were times in Hitch Village when I was picked at or bullied by boys three or even four years older than I. I always noticed these guys never bullied kids with brothers and sisters or a strong father figure in the home. There was even a time when an older boy tore down our screen door because my mother, who was having a party, would not let him into our house. This guy really thought he was a big man by belittling a woman and her 12-year-old son in front of the entire neighborhood. I was teased about the incident for months.

Financially, a father's absence is a crunch to a single mom and her children. I learned at an early age that money did not come easy. When I was old enough, probably about ten, I learned to hustle by selling soda water bottles and carrying grocery bags from the supermarket. A couple of years later, I started caddying at the Savannah Golf Club, making anywhere from four to six dollars for carrying a golf bag on my shoulder for eighteen holes on Saturday mornings and sometimes Sundays. Many times I would carry two bags for nine holes or caddy twice in one day (36 holes) and make about ten to twelve dollars. That was a ton of money in the 1960's. I could pay for lunch for the week at school, give my mama a dollar or two, lay away a pair of Converse All Stars shoes and still have enough to go see a movie, buy a RC Cola, a sweet roll, and a quarter's worth of boneless ham. It helped, but it did not take the place of the financial support that the father is supposed to give his family. In tenth and eleventh grades I bagged groceries at the M& M supermarket. In my senior year, I cooked short order meals at Shoney's Big Boy Restaurant. I worked at Union Camp, then International Paper for a year after graduating from high school, always helping my mother to meet the bills. But then I started slipping into darkness. I was very sad on the inside. Something was wrong: this was not who I was supposed to be at this point in my life. There was no peace within. I needed purpose in my life. There was no love around me; only judgment and criticism. I could find no strength, no hope, and no instruction.

Proverbs 1:8-9 says, *"Listen, my son, to your father's instruction and do not forsake your mother's teaching. They will be a garland to grace your head and a chain to adorn your neck."* This scripture alone proves that the home is not complete without the father's instruction and the mother's teaching.

When Death Takes Daddy From The Home

The untimely death of the father can be devastating to a wife and her children, especially if he was the sole bread winner. If that father did not put things in order such as life insurance, retirement plans and other investments, his family will suffer tremendously. Suddenly, the widow is faced with the reality of going out and getting a job to support her family. The children's lives will change also because they will find themselves with less supervision and more freedom to make the wrong choices. That mother must find a way to support her children and at the same time keep them from being enticed into slavery by the devil.

In the Book of II Kings 4:1-4,7, there is an account of a woman who lost her husband and found herself in great need. *"The wife of a man from the company of the prophets cried out to Elisha, your servant my husband is dead, and you know that he revered the Lord. But now his creditor is coming to take my two boys as his slaves." Elisha replied to her, "how can I help you? Tell me, what do you have in your house?" Your servant has nothing there at all," she said, "except a little oil." Elisha said go around and ask all your neighbors for empty jars. Don't ask for just a few. Then, go inside and shut the door behind you and your sons. Pour oil into all the jars, and as each is filled, put it to one side." She went and told the man of God, and he said, "Go, sell the oil and pay your debts. You and your sons can live on what is left."*

This mother, because of her spiritual relationship with God, had the resources and the faith to endure and not let the death of her husband affect her nor her children negatively. In many cases it's just the opposite, and the mother and her children cannot recover financially from the loss of the father. Families sometimes lose their homes and their cars, even though they have a relationship with God.

So, no matter the reason for the father's absence, that home will be affected negatively in many cases. Regardless of the mother's stability, the family still suffers when the father is gone.

Chapter Six

Breaking The Pattern

The word of the Lord came to me: What do you people mean by quoting this proverb about the land of Israel: "The fathers eat sour grapes, and the children's teeth are set on edge?" (Ezekiel 18:1-2)

For generations, sons have repeated the sins of their fathers. They have fathered children and left them to be raised by their mothers, another relative, or foster care. Their fathers were absent and never took the time to fill the void in their lives. This void sometimes created an attitude of disconcern: "My child will be all right without me there because I survived without a father."

Mitchell Landsberg of the Associated Press wrote a column in April 1995 entitled "Fatherless America: Families Today Often Headed By a Woman." Landsberg stated, "Somewhere on the road from *Ozzie and*

Harriet to *Murphy Brown* and *Newt's Boys'
Town,* America lost something."

David Blankenhorn thinks he knows what it
is: Fatherhood. According to this author,
"Fatherhood," is "a social role that obligates
men to their biological offspring;" and "the key
of the emergence of the human family and
ultimately, of human civilization." Beneath
these phrases lies the rather sharp point of
Blankenhorn's book, *Fatherless America:
Confronting Our Most Urgent Social Problem.*
His argument is that many things that is wrong
with America can be traced to the separation of
children from their biological fathers.

"Fatherlessness is the most harmful
demographic trend of this generation," he
writes. "It is the leading cause of the decline in
the well-being of children. It is also the engine
driving our most urgent social problems, from
crime to adolescent pregnancy to child sexual
abuse to domestic violence against woman."

These effects are especially intensified
among the boys that are left fatherless. Many of
them never grow up. They lack guidance and
discipline which are keys to adequate

development. All cultures want the same thing: males who are joy-filled, compassionate, and self-disciplined by the time they reach the age of twenty-one. This is where God-fearing, participating fathers come in. This is where we need to break the pattern.

Most boys flourish when they are given "attention, supervision, direction and responsibilities," states Tom Barton in the *Savannah Morning News.*

In the article, "Boys to Men: Society Is Failing Males," Barton argues that once boys reach a certain age, usually ten or eleven, they separate from their mothers and need their fathers. "It's a guy thing," he writes. Society used to make sure that boys knew how to be men and girls knew how to be women. We don't do that anymore.

They Need their Fathers

All children, not just the boys, need their fathers in order to become well-rounded and productive citizens. They need fathers who love God, who love their children, and have turned to the ways of God. The pattern they used to live by will not work anymore. Our children are perishing before our eyes. Fathers must now take charge and break all the negative, life-destroying patterns that were handed down by generations of fathers before them.

Fathers must allow themselves to be trained by God Himself. Fathers must allow themselves to get full of His Word and catch on fire through the Holy Spirit of God. Then fathers will be able to model scripture for their children as described in Proverbs 6:20-23b, *"My son, keep your father's commands and do not forsake your mother's teaching. Bind them upon your heart forever; fasten them around your neck. When you walk, they will guide you; when you sleep, they will watch over you, when you awake, they will speak to you. For these commands are a lamp and this teaching is a light."*

When fathers are trained by God, they can model scripture found in Proverbs 4:1-7, *"Listen my sons, to a father's instruction. Pay attention and gain understanding. I give you sound learning so do not forsake my teaching.*

Dennis L. Aikens

When I was a boy in my father's house, still tender and an only child of my mother, he taught me and said, lay hold of my words with all your hearts. Keep my commands and you will live. Get wisdom, get understanding; do not forget my words or swerve from them. Do not forsake wisdom, and she will protect you; love her, and she will watch over you. Wisdom is supreme; therefore, get wisdom. Though it cost all you have, get understanding."

Any pattern that offends, stifles, curses, or misinforms another can only be broken by the word of God and a love for God. Understanding the love that God has for us is to help us understand why we must break away from anything that does not represent Godliness. Neglecting your children, leaving your children to be raised only by their mother or someone else is not Godliness. God will never leave us or forsake us.

Fathers everywhere must look at the present condition of our society and say to themselves: "I must do whatever it takes to get in order with God so that I can get my house in order." Fathers must get their house in order, even if their children live outside their home. They must become a constant in the lives of their children. It is never too late to change the way you do things, especially if that change will produce positive effects in the lives of our children. Most children would welcome this change with open arms, right now.

There is a whole generation of children seeking direction and guidance. There are countless numbers of children looking for someone to love them. Children who do not know their father often pretend that they do not want to be disciplined nor want structure in their life; often we believe them. But I disagree. Children want authority and discipline to become a part of their lives, even if these elements are not yet a part of their known vocabulary.

Tragically, many of our children never knew the proper balance of love and discipline after entering the world from their mother's womb. All they ever knew was punishment— sometimes in the form of harsh beatings—for every bad thing they ever did. These children were rarely rewarded or praised for the good things they did. It was never explained why they were being punished, and many children were never properly encouraged to do better so they would not have to face the same results. These children were not taught options to their negative behavior.

The greatest encouragement that we can give our children is the same kind that God addresses us with in Hebrews 12:5-11: *"And you have forgotten that word of encouragement that addresses you as sons*: *'My son, do not make light of the Lord's discipline, and do not lose heart when he rebukes you, because the Lord disciplines those He loves, and punishes everyone he accepts as a son." Endure hardship as discipline; God is treating you as sons. For what son is not disciplined by his father? If you are not disciplined (and everyone undergoes discipline), then you are illegitimate children and not true sons. Moreover, we have all had human fathers who disciplined us and we respected them for it. How much more should we submit to the father of our spirits and live: Our fathers disciplined us for a little while as they thought best; but*

God disciplines us for our good, that we may share in His holiness. No discipline seems pleasant at the time, but is painful. Later on, however, it produces a harvest of righteousness and peace for those who have been trained by it."

Pattern Breakers Are Needed

Our children need Pattern Breakers so they too can become Pattern Breakers. Pattern Breakers are fathers who are determined not to be another statistic—another deadbeat dad; another dad missing in action; another weak man who has nothing but excuses for why he is not in place in the lives of his children. "I can't get along with your mother." "She won't let me see my children." "They moved to another city, so I never get to see them anymore." These are horrible excuses.

A Pattern Breaker would put an end to that mess and say: "Where there is a will, there is a way. I will find a way to take care of and to see my children. No devil in hell will keep me from being a positive influence in the lives of my children. My children are an inheritance from God and I will be blessed by them. But I must bless them with the sacrifice I make to live in the image of God and I must bless them with my presence in their life."

A Pattern Breaker loves his children and refuses to let Satan and the world swallow them up and destroy them right before his very eyes. A Pattern Breaker set standards not only for his children, but also for other future Pattern Breakers to follow.

It's desperation time. We must change the patterns of fatherhood by any means necessary. All it takes is a few fathers who have done it wrong for so long to say, "I will break this pattern of leaving, losing, and destroying our children."

Chapter Seven

Absent, But Still In the House

For though I am absent from you in body I am present with you in spirit and delight to see how orderly you are and how firm your faith in Christ is. (Colossians 2:5)

It is a tragedy to see so many fathers living physically in the home with their children, yet spiritually far away in terms of training, nurturing and molding their children. They are missing in action because their children do not even know they exist except to see them around the home first thing in the morning and maybe sometimes at night, when it is time to retire for the evening.

Children, especially younger children, are always asking about Daddy: "When is daddy coming home, is daddy coming to P.T.A meeting, why don't daddy ever go to church with us?" Older children often remind their father that they were not there for them and that their father acted as if he did not care or did not love them. Fathers need to be reminded that the children growing up in their homes, right before their eyes, are their seeds. These children are the fathers growing up all over again. So if you love yourself, you must love your reproduction of yourself. For they are your seed, your children.

It all begins with paying attention to your children at every stage while growing up in the home. As fathers, we must always be involved with our children's lives. What activities are they involved in? What are some of the things they are thinking? Who do they listen to and hang out with? These are things we must know.

Knowing what's going on with your children can prevent many bad things from happening in their lives, and it can also prevent them from hating and resenting you when they become adults. If King David had been a discerning father—knowing what was going on with his children, knowing what was in their hearts and their minds—he would have been able to prevent one son, Amnon, from raping his sister Tamar and preventing another son, Absalom, from killing his brother, Amnon. This entire story is recorded in II Samuel 13:1-39.

King David's son Absalom did not stop with murder; he continued until he desired his father's throne, and plotted a conspiracy to entice the Israelites to worship him as King. This conspiracy caused David to flee for his life because he realized the hearts of the people were with Absalom, his son. This account is recorded in II Samuel 15:1-37.

All of these things happened because a father was not intimately involved in the hearts and minds of his children. Our children cannot see us live one kind of life and teach and preach another kind. Amnon had his father's lustful spirit and Absalom had his father's murdering and covetous spirit. The only things they saw while their father was present in the house were negative things. So the spiritual father they needed was absent even though he was in the house raising his children.

Dennis L. Aikens

Fathers Must Become Living Sacrifices

"Therefore, I urge you, brothers, in view of God's mercy, to offer your bodies as living sacrifices, holy and pleasing to God—this is your spiritual act of worship. Do not conform any longer to the pattern of this world, but be ye transformed by the renewing of your mind. Then you will be able to test and approve what God's will is - His good, pleasing and perfect will." (Romans 12:1-2)

In order for fathers to sacrifice their lives to God and to the proper management of their children, they must first understand what it means to break the patterns that have been set by themselves, by fathers before them, and by fathers before them.

The Bible says in this passage from Romans that you can no longer conform or go along with those ways or patterns because they do not represent fathers or men as being in the image of God. God will not treat his children the way some fathers treat theirs. We cannot fall short any longer because we are misrepresenting

God. We must now become the standard instead of the norm. God is expecting fathers to come up. We have been too far down for too long.

If we are in the business of pleasing God and not Satan, then we must test ourselves to see if we are breaking patterns and setting new standards. We must be able to pass the test, to see if we are conformed, if we are convinced, and if we approve of what God wants us to do in our life. We must begin seeing with our spiritual eyes.

It is a fact that what God wants to do in our life is His good, pleasing and perfect will. Our sacrifice becomes the world's blessing because the fruit from the sacrifice is bountiful—better-behaved children, children with high self-esteem and confidence, and children with vision and a mission. Finally, our sacrifice produces children who can take their time in childhood and not have to grow up too fast.

Dennis L. Aikens

Guess Who's Coming to Dinner?

We as fathers cannot make any more excuses like, "If I do not work, this family won't eat," or "I am just too tired to go to the recital or game." These excuses are ancient, and they are not acceptable. If there is a will to do better and to do what is right by your children and family, then there is definitely a way. A good plan won't hurt, either.

A man with a plan says, "I will participate in the children's activities once a week, or once every two weeks." A man with a plan says, "I will be home for dinner two days a week, even if I have to cut back on my second job. Two or three hours every Saturday, we will do something as a family." When you have such a plan, you will see your children becoming excited and looking forward to these events—a wonderful thing to see. It is because you as the father and head of the house have become consistent and attentive to your children's needs. A time before they said, "Yes, I have a daddy, but he is never around even though he lives with us." But now they are saying, "I have a mama and a daddy and we do a lot of stuff together." Children who have fathers in the home need their love, encouragement, and strength—and they need them to know what's going on in their lives. They are crying out. "Daddy, I am over here, come see about me."

Chapter Eight

Setting The Pace

So let my Lord go on ahead of his servant, while I move along slowly at the pace of the droves before me and that of the children until I come to my Lord in Seir. (Genesis 33:14)

Management and rearing of children are tasks very important to God. Children that are reared in the fear of the Lord and who are developed properly will eventually become weapons for God in the war against Satan and his plans to destroy the plans of God. They become treasure before the Lord. Anything that is a treasure must be protected and secured, and it must be preserved because it is very valuable. For the Lord says in Deuteronomy 7:6, "*For you are a people holy to the Lord your God. The Lord your God has chosen you out of all the peoples on the face of the earth to be his people, his treasured possession.*"

Now we know that we all are treasures before the Lord, and our children are also treasures. We must be careful lest we neglect this fact. According to Jacob in Genesis 33:5c, God has to be embarrassed by how some of us as parents, especially fathers, have taken the task of caring for children so lightly. It is time to set the pace, to slow down enough so that our children can keep up with us as we navigate them to a point where they can take the lead for themselves. Breaking the pattern of not being there is the first step. The next step is to set the pace, give the guidance, protection, and resources.

In Genesis 33 when Jacob and his brother Esau had made peace with one another over Jacob's deception of Esau, Jacob offered his brother a gift of livestock because he recognized that God had been extremely good to him. Esau eventually accepted it after Jacob persisted. Then Esau said in Genesis 33:12, "*Let us be on our way; I'll accompany you.*" But Jacob said to him, "*My Lord knows that the children are tender and that I must care for the ewes and cows that are nursing their young. If*

67

they are driven hard just one day, all the animals will die. So go on ahead of me while I move along slowly at the pace of the droves before me and that of the children, until I come to my Lord in Seir."

This is what God is saying to fathers; slow down and back up to where the children are. For they are tender, inexperienced, and undeveloped. They need you to come down to their level and slowly take them to your level, if it is at a level with God.

There were times in Hitch Village when I had to act older than I needed to. I was moving too fast. At age eleven, for example, I sold bottles of whiskey and shots to customers coming to my house because my mother was recovering from a hangover and was too sick to answer the door. My mother had a bout with alcoholism back then, but I thank God she has been delivered a long time ago and now saved and born again for 20 years. I was growing up too fast. I would leave liquor at the bottom of the bottles for me and my friends to drink. I stole cigarettes from my mother and her friends and I would even peep into the bathroom windows of some of the younger, beautiful mothers of that time. Because my house was out of order, I was out of order. My mother did the best she could to shelter me and to keep me from getting too deep into the streets. She worked hard to provide for me and to keep the lights on and a roof over our heads, but because she was still dealing with a lot of hurt and pain, she never was able to accomplish the things she wanted for herself such as more education, a career, and possibly a husband. She didn't marry until I was 19 years old. By then I was deep into the streets. All because a dream was broken, there was no one there to set the pace. Therefore, I was out of sync and in trouble. I was heading toward substance abuse.

Looked Good for a While

In elementary and middle school, I lived in Hitch Village and I was very active in sports and academics. I was an "A" student through the eighth grade and excelled every year in football and basketball. I had potential and dreams, but tragedy struck. My mother's twin sister died in a car accident in June 1969, and this led us to move out of Hitch Village.

After living in Hitch Village for seven years, I was just beginning to conquer "the Village." I was an active player on Hitch Village's 13 and under basketball team. My team won the 1969 Eastside City Recreational Basketball Championship in March 1969. At Sol. C. Johnson High School I was an eighth grade honor roll student six consecutive marking periods. My future was looking good. I began ninth grade at Savannah High School for one marking period. Then we moved and I was transferred to another high school, Beach High School. Eventually, I graduated from Jenkins High School in 1973. There were only seven public high schools in Savannah and I was a student at four of them within four years. However, my whole world changed with the third relocation. The streets began to draw me from my home, which had become even more chaotic. My home was a station to many hurting people, including my mother and three cousins, who were the children of my mother's deceased twin sister. I found out then that hurting people hurt people.

By eleventh grade, I started using drugs. If I ever needed a strong man around to guide me, challenge me, and get me back on track, I sure did need one then. I needed someone to back up, slow down and come to where I was. I was lost and on my way to hell. My mother was still dealing with her own issues, so she could not hear my cry. There was no father to be found, because I found out my father was shot dead in Florida when I was about eleven years old. And I only saw him once in my entire life.

Get With Me

In order to successfully set the pace for our children and get them where God wants them to be, we as fathers must get with God. Wherever God is, we must get there.

Isaiah 55:8-9 says, "*For my thoughts are not your thoughts, neither are your ways my ways, declares the Lord. As the heavens are higher than the earth, so are my ways higher than your ways and my thoughts than your thoughts.*"

We must realize that we can never become God, but we must also realize that we can have His ways. We can live holy, and we can live right and pleasing in the sight of God.

Philippians 4:8 says, "*Finally, brothers, whatever is true, whatever is noble, whatever is right, whatever is pure, whatever is lovely, whatever is admirable—if anything is excellent or praise worthy—think about such things. Whatever you have learned or received or heard from me, or seen in me—put it into practice and the God of peace will be with you.*"

In other words, God is saying to fathers that in order to get with me, you must think how I think and do and say what I do and say. Everything we need concerning raising our children, setting the proper pace for them based upon each child's personality and abilities, and providing for them is in the word of God. Jesus has all the answers for us, especially in the Gospels and the Epistles of Paul. The word of God is the best road map or book of instruction there is for developing children.

Our children are watching us and in most cases whatever we do, they do and whatever we say, they say. They repeat our actions and our thoughts. Once we have sown bad seeds into our children, it is hard to purge them. That is why it is so important that we make our best impressions upon them when they are young so that when they grow up the lessons shall not depart from them.

Who's Influencing Whom?

In setting the pace for our children, they need someone who is strong enough to influence them spiritually in the midst of all the peer pressure they face to act and look a certain way. A father who truly loves God and who seeks after God's own heart will have great influence on his children. His children will see the characteristics in him that they will need at some point in their life if they desire to please God.

These are characteristics such as faith, commitment, love, long suffering and perseverance, meekness and humility, boldness and determination. These are qualities that God expects and honors in a man because these are the qualities of God. Two other qualities or characteristics that fathers must possess if they are to become the ultimate influence in their children's lives, are praying to God and praising God.

Praying is communication between God and man. The Bible says man ought to always pray. Prayer allows God to see inside your heart and mind based on how often and how effectively you pray. Praising God is the same as recognizing how great and awesome God is, and honoring Him for being the creator that He is. Praising God is also appreciating God, giving Him thanks for all that He does and will do for us. Our children must be influenced greatly in the areas of praying to and praising God.

We cannot allow our children to influence us by not wanting to receive spiritual guidance and instructions. Many of our children get to an age where they do not want to be bothered and want to hear nothing being said to them. But the devil is a liar. We have been charged to make disciples of all nations, including our own, according to Matthew 28:18-20, by Jesus Himself. We cannot influence the world and forget about our children, and we cannot allow our children to influence us away from influencing them about the ways of God.

It is our responsibility as fathers to lead our families through the wilderness into the Promised Land. Now there will come times when we will have to slow down and not drive our little ones too hard because they may tire, fall away from the family, and perish in the wilderness. So many of our children, all over this country, are dying because fathers are not shepherding the flock that God entrusted to them. But God is raising up a new generation of fathers who will obey and who will set the house in order.

Chapter Nine

The 21st Century Father

Dear children, do not let anyone lead you astray. He who does what is right is righteous, just as he is righteous. He who does what is sinful is of the devil, because the devil has been sinning from the beginning. The reason the Son of God appeared was to destroy the devil's work. No one who is born of God will continue to sin, because God's seed remains in Him; he cannot go on sinning because he has been born of God. This is how we know who the children of God are and who the children of the devil are: Anyone who does not do what is right is not a child of God, nor is anyone who does not love his brother. (I John 3:7-10)

The questions that the 21st century father must answer are: "Am I doing the right thing, and am I a child of God or a child of the devil?" Fathers today cannot for the sake of their children ignore these questions. There is a great demand for fathers in the 21st century who love the Lord with all their heart, mind, strength, and soul.

It's time for Superfly, Mack Daddy, drug-pushing, corner-hanging, back-stabbing, won't-look-for-a-job, child-deserting, selfish, womanizing, and won't-grow-up fathers to stand up and be the fathers that God ordained us to be back in the beginning when he created Adam in His own image.

There was a time in the late 1970's when I fell into one of these categories. I was trying to finish college, on a four-year government grant at Armstrong State College, when I had my first son out of wedlock with a beautiful young woman, Beverly, who would eventually become my wife. I was broke and could not find a job that would not interfere with my quest for a college degree. I was already abusing drugs, but then I started dealing drugs to make ends meet. I was now a fifth year college student with no grant money. I was now out of mother's house and living in my own apartment. I needed rent money, milk for the baby, books for college, and most of all I needed my degree. I didn't let anything stand in my way.

I was wrong and lost, but I did manage to graduate from college with a double Bachelors of Arts degree in Marketing Management and Management. Man, what a feeling that was in June 1980 to march across that stage! But my mess was not over. I could not find a job. I possessed two college degrees and I could not find a job in my home city. I tried Atlanta and Jacksonville, IBM and Xerox, but no one gave me a look. I kept abusing drugs and things got worse—so bad until one day I knew I was at rock bottom.

One of my best friends and I almost had a shoot-out in my house over some drug money I owed him. He had a pistol and was standing in the door at the bottom of the stairs of my second story apartment. He never knew to this day that I also had my pistol in place in case he began shooting at me. That incident damaged one of the best friendships I ever had. I was out of touch with God and I was in the middle of a generational curse that I had to break. But somewhere back in my lineage there were preachers and businessmen. I knew deep within me I needed to find a way to get right with God. Although I was a church-goer all my life, I was not connected to Christ. So, in July 1981 I gave my life to Christ at the age of twenty-six. Glory to God, I have not looked back since.

To the world, it sometimes appears that God wasted His time creating man in His own image and giving him dominion to rule over the entire earth including the fish of the sea, the birds of the air, the livestock and all creatures that move along the ground. But God will never change his mind, according to Numbers 23:19. For the Bible says in this text, "*God is not a man, that he should lie, nor a son of man, that he should change his mind.*" God will do whatever he said he was going to do and he will fulfill that which he promised.

Now it is up to man to fulfill their end of the bargain. One man at a time must begin to get in order with God's ways and desires, and then it will become contagious. Men and fathers everywhere will begin to walk towards the Word because the world can only offer them curses and death. God will not hold back his judgment on those who refuse to hear his voice and his cry, for the last trumpet will be blowing soon. The Bible clearly tells us that we are living in the last days.

In this new century we need fathers who have found their rightful place with God to become mentors and standard setters for those who are still lost and out of place. Sacrifices must be made to build up the area of fatherhood in the body of Christ. Older men must not only tell how it should be done, they must also live how it should be done.

Paul told his spiritual son Titus in the Book of Titus to set the church in order on the Island of Crete. He told Titus to straighten out in the church what was left unfinished, according to Titus 1:5. He directed Titus to appoint elders in every town and the elder must be blameless, the husband of but one wife, a man whose children believe and is not open to the charge of being wild and disobedient. In the 2nd chapter of Titus, beginning at the first verse, Paul compels his son to teach sound doctrine, which is the body of truth taught by Jesus. Then, Paul writes, teach the older men to be temperate, worthy of respect, self-controlled, and sound in faith, in love and endurance. Finally, in verse 6, Paul calls on the young men to be self-controlled and in everything set an example by doing good. Men and fathers must be taught through the word of God what is expected of them.

When King David found out where he belonged with God and how much God meant to him, he made sure when he was old that he taught his son Solomon about the ways of God and the benefits of keeping all the commands and the decrees of God. In I Kings 2:2-4, David charged Solomon and said: "*I am about to go the way of all the earth, so be strong, show yourself a man, and observe what the Lord your God requires: walk in his ways and keep his decrees and commands, his laws and requirements, as written in the law of Moses, so that you may prosper in all you do and wherever you go, and that the Lord may keep his promise to me: If your descendants watch how they live, and if they walk faithfully before me with all their heart and soul, you will never fail to have a man on the throne of Israel.*"

That was a father teaching his son how to love God and keep his ways in order for him to be a good father and leader.

Finding Isaiah

For two decades, I never knew my father's family except for the one day that my father tried to take me to meet his mother. The paternal side of me was empty. I had no knowledge, no information of my paternal family. The roots of a child are so important for that child to know because they help determine who they will become. Finally, at the age of twenty, I met a young man who would become the key to my wholeness.

We met in First Bryan Baptist Church in Yamacraw Village in Savannah, Georgia. He was a talented, scholarly young man with tremendous charisma. He was an educator and later would become a minister of the Gospel of Jesus Christ. We became very close friends. One day I just happened to mention that my surname was Boles, the name I was baptized under, but I went by the name Aikens. He was fascinated by the fact that his last name was the same as my surname, Boles, and the fact that we had so many similar biological features. He began to ask questions. Coincidentally, one of his sisters and I had also become close because we were drama students together in college. They began to ask their older family members questions about my father's name. Then he would take me on drives to Richmond Hill, Georgia, the birthplace of the Boles and Williams family.

Finally, we discovered that my father was their father's nephew. My grandfather was their father's oldest sibling. This was the beginning of wholeness for the first time in my life. I was told that my great-grandfather was a mighty preacher and businessman in his day. He was a man who founded churches. God had sent an angel to guide me into His perfect will for my life and I thank God everyday for "finding Isaiah."

King David was not always perfect, but once he became a Pattern Breaker he was able to pivot and become a pacesetter. He set his house in order and made new standards for himself and his family to follow.

The 21st century father must establish new order in his life and become a positive role model for his children and other fathers around him. It is essential that he learn God's will for his life now, so that he can get in place as a member of the body and that he can become a light to the world.

21st century fathers cannot get caught up in some of the traditions of old, because some traditions will not allow God to move freely in the body of Christ. This is true, especially, when it comes to reaching the younger generation. God is the same yesterday, today, and forever more. But God has to change his methods and make adjustments in order to reach each generation. Each generation faces new obstacles, new influences, and different demonic activities and forces. The devil keeps up with the times and the changes. He is aware of the new drugs and new devices to destroy God's people. So God must do likewise. He must make changes to get into the enemy's camp and draw out recruits who will then go back into the enemy's camp and win souls for Jesus.

Some traditions of men do not accept the use of contemporary Christian music and dancing in the church but yet this form of worship can lure our children from the devil's charm. We need to embrace our youth with their dreadlocks, body-piercing, tatoos, and hip-hop instead of condemning them. Let's love them, for God loves us all inspite of ourselves. God is doing a new thing on earth and He is drawing more men in from the world than ever before. But when they come in, He needs leaders who can equip them and train them to become 21st century fathers who will then turn around and train and equip their children to love and serve God. God will change their appearance, if their appearance needs changing. For the time is definitely now to make a move on the devil's plan: which is to destroy the seed of God. This seed, of course, is man.

If he can destroy man, he will destroy fathers, and then children will grow up half empty.

Dennis L. Aikens

Chapter Ten

It's Time

The Lord our God said to us at Horeb, "you have stayed long enough at this mountain. Break camp and advance into the hill country of the Amorites; go to all the neighboring peoples in the Arabah, in the mountains, in the western foothills, in the Negev and along the coast, to the land of the Canaanites and to Lebanon, as far as the great river, the Euphrates. See, I have given you this land. Go in and take possession of the land that the Lord swore he would give to your fathers—to Abraham, Isaac and Jacob— and to their descendants after them." (Deuteronomy 1:6-8)

There is a mountain facing our society and it is mighty. It is the crucial issue of fatherlessness. Fatherhood is shrinking by the day, and too many young lives are being marred by paternal abandonment, according to Marjorie Williams, columnist for the

Washington Post. She wrote in a recent column, at present, forty percent of all children and almost eighty percent of black children can expect to spend some significant portion of their childhood in a home without a father. Williams states that while the exact effects are still a furiously contested issue, it is impossible to deny at least some connection between several of our worst pathologies, especially child poverty and youth violence, and our culture's devaluation of fatherhood. Williams continued to note that the black community has increasingly tried to tackle this issue openly, noting that while non-marital births to African-American women are now declining, they still occur at almost twice the rate of unwed parenthood among whites.

A 1998 conference on African-American fathers at Morehouse College in Atlanta, Georgia urged civil rights organizations to recognize a crisis in African-American fatherhood, and resolved that reversing the trend of father absence must rise to the top of the agenda for African-Americans and for the nation.

Dennis L. Aikens

Breaking Camp

God has declared that too many fathers have been on the mountain of fatherlessness for too long, and it is time to break camp and be about our father's business. We know that there is a problem with absent fathers. We know we need to break the pattern, and we know we need to set the pace and establish new standards of fatherhood. The next step is here. Just do it.

Implement the actions required to please God. Develop and prepare our children for life and everything that life holds. It is time to rebuke ourselves as absent fathers and pay attention to the needs of our children. Not one child born from the mother's womb asked to come into the world. But many find themselves facing the world without paternal covering.

It is time for us to end that scene. It is time for fathers to lead their children to the Promised Land, a place where they are in the will of God. God can give the perpetual rest. Our children are tired of living fast. They are tired of running to survive, and tired of acting bad to get attention. They need fathers who will take charge of their lives and give them purpose and direction.

Proof and precedents have shown that many fathers are not fatherhood material. They are biological dads who lack the qualities needed to love, cherish and relate to their children. But despite their inefficiencies, their children must get to know them in order for them to be whole. Children must know where they come from: why they look the way they look; act the way they act; think the way they think. They need to know why they were born with their particular abilities, talents, and skills. They need to know why they possess certain bad qualities, bad habits, and bad dispositions. How will they know what to fix, if they don't know where it came from? That's reason enough for absent fathers to realize that it's time to let their children know them, so they can know themselves.

Who Is Willing To Go First?

Isaiah 6:5-8, the word of God says, "*Woe to me! I cried. I am ruined! For I am a man of unclean lips, and I live among a people of unclean lips, and my eyes have seen the king, the lord Almighty. Then one of the seraphs flew to me with a live coal in his hand, which he had taken with tongs from the altar. With it he touched my mouth and said, see, this has touched your lips; your quilt is taken away and your sin atoned for. Then I heard the voice of the Lord saying, "whom shall I send? And who will go for us? And I said, 'Here am I, send me'. ""*

It is time for absent fathers to go back and be where God wants them to be; in place and in their children's lives. Fathers must return from exile, from the captivity of the enemy, because of their sin of not taking care of the lambs of God. For the babies are tender, and they need caring for. They need constant attention. Their lives need to be touched by someone who knows, loves, and lives for God. Jesus himself was very adamant about how the children needed to be loved and received. Once again, in Mark 10:13-16, people were bringing little children to Jesus to have Him touch them, but the disciples rebuked them. When Jesus saw this, He was indignant. He said to them, "*Let the little children come to me, and do not hinder them, for the kingdom of God belongs to such as these. I tell you the truth, anyone who will not receive the kingdom of God like a little child will never enter it.*" *And he took the children in his arms, put his hands on them and blessed them.*

Because God is a God of mercy, He will allow us to prove to him that we will do what He desires, though we may have been punished for our sins. He wants us to humble ourselves, pray and seek his face, and turn from our wicked ways. II Chronicles 7:14: "*then he can hear from heaven, forgive our sins and heal our land.*" If we are sincere about restoring relationships with our children and are willing, "to trust in the Lord with all our heart and lean not to our own understanding: in all your ways acknowledge him, and he will make or direct our paths straight." (Proverbs 3:5-6.)

This business of fatherlessness is serious business to God. It is not a joke, and it is not funny to Him. Satan is trying to destroy a whole generation of children because some men—whom God made in his image to be kings, warriors, and royal priests of a holy nation have dropped the ball. They left their babies at the mercy of the devil, and the devil has no mercy. I Peter 5:8b says: "*Your enemy the devil prowls around like a roaring lion looking for someone to devour.*" He wants to make God, our father, look bad. That's why he attacks the seed, man, and keeps him out of place with God. If he is successful with that, many men will be out of place with their own seed, their children, and leave them unguarded.

I previously discussed how Jesus gave one of the most serious mandates for pastors. I also believe this mandate applies to fathers. It was given after Jesus arose from the dead and after Peter had sinned and denied Jesus three times. *When they had finished eating, Jesus said to Simon Peter, "Simon son of John, do you truly love me more than these?" "Yes, Lord," he said, "You know that I love you." Jesus said, "Feed my lambs." Again Jesus said, "Simon son of John, do you truly love me?" "Yes, Lord, you know that I love you." "Take care of*

*my sheep." The third time he said to him,
"Simon son of John, do you love me?" He
said, "Lord you know all things; you know that
I love you." Jesus said, "feed my sheep."* John
21:15-17

There are far too many hungry lambs
walking our streets with no one to feed them.
God is reviving the mandate that Jesus gave to
Peter, and he is giving the mandate to absent
fathers everywhere. "Feed my sheep."

Glory to God, Amen.

Dennis L. Aikens

"WORD FIRST" CHRISTIAN CHURCH
AUDIO CASSETTE MINISTRY
Dennis L. Aikens, Pastor
2409 Alfed Street
Savannah, GA 31408
912-964-7819

$3.00 per tape

Your Name:_____Date:_____

Message Title	Date	Scriptures	Check ✔
The Principles of Forgiveness **(Part 2 – Forgive and Be Forgiven)** (Pastor Dennis L. Aikens)	2nd Sun 3/12/00	Matthew 18:21-27	
Developing Partner/Covenant Relationship With God **(Part 1 – Let's Start With Abraham)**	Wed 3/22/00	Genesis 12:1-4, 15:1-6	
Developing Partner/Covenant Relationship With God **(Part 2 – The Two Seeds of Abraham)**	4th Sun 3/26/00	Genesis 12:1-3 Genesis 15:1-6 Galatians 3:25-29	

Message Title	Date	Scriptures	Check ✔
Developing Partner/Covenant Relationship With God (**Part 3- Opposites Attract**)	Wed 3/29/00	Genesis 26:1-17, 26-31 Romans 15:1-4	
Developing Partner/Covenant Relationship With God (**Part 4 – The Covenant Was Made To Get Rid of Our Weaknesses**)	1st Sun 4/2/00	Roman 15:1-5 Ephesians 2:10	
Let The Spirit Have Its Way	Thurs 4/13/00	Matthew 12:15-18, 22-32	
Murmuring (**"Complaining for The Last Time"**)	Wed 12/1/99	Numbers 13:21-33, 14:1-18	
Murmuring (**"All Authority Is God Given, So Why Are Your Complain-ing"**)	Wed 12/8/99	Numbers 16:1-26	
When The Thrill Is Gone	2nd Sun 12/12/99	Jeremiah 2	

Dennis L. Aikens

Message Title	Date	Scriptures	Check ✔
Mercy Suits My Case **"The Good Samaritan"**	Wed 12/15/99		
Murmuring (**"All Authority Is God Given, So Why Are Your Complain- ing"**)	Wed 12/22/99	Numbers 16:1-4	
Tithing 2000 (Understanding Where It Came From)	Wed 1/05/00	Numbers 18:20-32	
Redefining Our Roles: What Part Do You Play?	2nd Sun 1/09/00	I Corinthians 12:12-27	
Speaking the Mystery (Min. Beverly Aikens)	Wed 1/12/00	Acts 1:5-8, 2:1-4 I Corinthians 14:2	
Dwelling In God's Shelter	Wed 9/22/99	Psalms 91	
The Just Shall Live By Faith	4th Sun 9/26/99	Galatians 3:1-26	
Distinguishing Spirits	Wed 10/6/99	I John 4:1-7	

Message Title	Date	Scriptures	Check ✔
God's Will for Your Life **Introduction to Series "Lord, I Heard You, I Just Didn't Listen"** (Sis. Beverly Aikens)	Wed 10/13/99		
Part 1 – Lord, I Heard… Didn't Listen (**"The Way of Balaam"**)	3rd Sun 10/17/99	Numbers 22, 23, 24, 25	
Wet… Had No Fire!	Wed 10/27/99	Acts 19:1-5, 11-20	
Part II – Lord, I Heard… Didn't Listen (**"The Error of Balaam"**)	5th Sun 10/31/99	Numbers 23:5-20	
Distinguishing Spirits, Part II	Wed 11/3/99	Acts 19:1-7, 11-16	
Part III – Lord, I Heard…Didn't Listen (**"Betrayed From the Inside, Destroyed From Within"**)	1st Sun 11/7/99	Numbers 25:1-9	

Dennis L. Aikens

Message Title	Date	Scriptures	Check ✔
Breaking the Pattern, Part I (Generational Curses)	2nd Sun 8/8/99	Ezekiel 18:1-21	
Breaking the Pattern, Part II (Be Ye Transformed)	Wed 8/11/99	II Kings 16:1-4, 18:1-8 Ezekiel 18:2-17	
God's Divine Order of the Family (Sis. Beverly Aikens)	3rd Sun 8/15/99	Colossians 3:15-25 Ephesians 5:22: 33	
There's a Better Way Than the Way You're Going Now	4th Sun 8/22/99	Matthew 7:13-4 John 10:7-10	
If It Don't Concern You, Leave It Alone	Wed 8/25/99	John 21:17-23 I Thessalonians 4:11, 12	
Faith Without Works Is Dead	5th Sun 8/29/99	James 2:14-17	
We Are All Ministers of Reconciliation	Wed 4/21/99	II Corinthians 5:10	
Without Holiness, How Can We Serve?	Fri 4/23/99 at Christ Memorial	Colossians 3:1-17	

Message Title	Date	Scriptures	Check ✔
Running in the Wrong Direction	Wed 4/28/99	Jonah 1:1-12	
To Be Absent From the Body, But Present With the Lord	Sat 5/1/99	Thessalonians 4:13-18	
Seek Ye First the Kingdom	1st Sun 5/2/99	Mark 10:17-31	
I'm Not Ashamed of the Gospel Part 1	Wed 5/5/99	Jude 1-9	
Hanna "2000" (Looking for Some Real Women)	2nd Sun 5/9/99	I Samuel 1:1-13	
I'm Not Ashamed of the Gospel Part 2, (Defending Your Faith)	Wed 5/12/99	Jude 3-5, 10-20	Not Avail.
Living By Faith and Not By Sight	3rd Sun 5/16/99	Hebrews 11	
It's Time	Wed 12/30/98	Deuteronomy 1:1-11	
Gifts That Are Never Opened, Parts 1 & 2	Wed 1/13/99 & Sat 1/17/99	I Corinthians 12:1-11	

99

Dennis L. Aikens

Message Title	Date	Scriptures	Check ✔
Gifts That Are Never Opened, Part 3	Wed 1/20/99	I Corinthians 13	
Gifts That Are Never Opened, Part 4	4th Sun 1/24/99	I Corinthians 14	
When The Praises Go Up Part 1	Wed 1/27/99	Psalms 34	
When The Praises Go Up Part 2	5th Sun 1/31/99	I Chronicles 16: 25	
When The Praises Go Up Part 3	Wed 2/3/99	Act 16:16-27	
The Anointing of God Must Flow Down, Part 1	Wed 2/17/99	Psalms 133 Ephesians 4:12-16	
The Anointing of God Must Flow Down, Part 2 (Stirring Up The Anointing)	3rd Sun 2/21/99	Psalms 133	
The Anointing of God Must Flow Down, Part 3 (Keep Your Eye On The Anointing)	Wed 2/24/99	I Kings 19:15-21 II Kings 2:1-15	
Discerning the Body (Holy Communion)	4th Sun 2/28/99	I Corinthians 11:17-30	
When the Disobedience of One Effects Us All, Part 1	Wed 3/3/99	Joshua 6:15-19, 7:1-12	

Message Title	Date	Scriptures	Check ✔
When the Disobedience of One Effects Us All, Part 2	1st Sun 3/7/99	Joshua 6:15-19, 7:1-12	
Giving God Your Best and Nothing Less, Part 1 (Tithing Principles)	Wed 3/10/99	Malachi 1:6-14	
Giving God Your Best and Nothing Less, Part 2 (Tithing Principles)	2nd Sun 3/14/99	Genesis 12:1-3, 14:14-20 Malachi 3:6-10	
Giving God Your Best and Nothing Less, Part 3 (Biblical Applications)	Wed 3/17/99	I Kings 17:7-14 Proverbs 3:5-10 Luke 21:1-4	
Go Back and Look Again	3rd Sun 3/21/99	James 1:19-25 Matthew 13:1-6	
On One Condition (Prosperity) Part I	Wed 4/7/99	Deuteronomy 28:1-14 Galatians 3	
You Are Out of Place (Redefining Our Roles)	3rd Sun 1/16/00	I Corinthians 3:1-9	
Now That You Are In Place, Here's the Plan	4th Sun 1/23/00	Romans 5:12-21	

Dennis L. Aikens

Message Title	Date	Scriptures	Check ✔
Tithing 2000 (**He Never Told Us to Stop**)	Wed 1/26/00	Hebrews 7:1-7	
Still Struggling With Sin	1st Sun 2/6/00	Romans 7:7-17	
Let The Spirit Have Its Way	2nd Sun 2/13/00	Matthew 12-15-32	
When All Hell Broke In Heaven	Wed 2/16/00	Isaiah 14:12-18	
Doing It With the Light On (Jesus is the Light)	4th Sun 2/27/00	John 3:17-31 John 8:12	
The Message of God's Kingdom	1st Sun 3/5/00	Matthew 13:1-13	
Open Sores and Bruised Egos (**Part 1 – Forgive and Be Forgiven**) (Min. Beverly Aikens)	Wed 3/8/00	Psalm 42:11 Isaiah 53:4-5 Psalm 9:1-14 Mark 11:25	

References

Blankenhorn, David, "Fatherless America: Confronting Our Most Urgent Social Problem", The Associated Press, April 17, 1995

Landsberg, Mitchell, "Fatherless America: Families Today Often Headed By A Woman" The Associated Press, April 17, 1995

Barton, Tom, "Boys to Men: Society Is Failing Males", Savannah Morning News Commentary, November 7, 1999, p. 15A

Williams, Majorie, Columnist, The Washington Post, "Focus should be on Jesse's daughter", 2001

Disciple's Study Bible, New International Version, Holman Bible Publishers, Nashville, 1988
American Heritage Dictionary of the English Language, New College Edition, Houghton and Mifflin, 1969,70,71,73,75,

Dennis L. Aikens

Special Thanks To:
Beverly A. Aikens
Elizabeth Hudson-Goff
Trudy E. Jones

Cover design
Miracle Graphics
Iesha Brown

About the Author

Dennis L. Aikens was born 3-25-55 in Savannah, Georgia to Barbara Aikens and Lewis Boles. He was educated in the public school system of Savannah. He graduated in 1980 from Armstrong State College (Now Armstrong Atlantic University) with a double business degree in marketing/management and management. He graduated in 1996 with a Master of Ministry and in 1997 with a Doctor of Ministry from Covington Theological Seminary. He is the pastor of Word First Christian Church and the agent/owner of Dennis L. Aikens Insurance Agency Inc. (State Farm Insurance) both in Savannah, Georgia. He is married to Beverly A. Aikens and they have four sons; Delandrian, Dennis Jr., Derrin and Derrick. They have one grandson, Jamarie.

www.ingramcontent.com/pod-product-compliance
Lightning Source LLC
Chambersburg PA
CBHW030339290526
45785CB00004B/1537